A SHORTER SHAKESPEARE

*O*thello

Illustrated by Cal Williams

MACMILLAN • USA

MACMILLAN
A Simon & Schuster Macmillan Company
1633 Broadway
New York, NY 10019

First published in 1996 by
Appletree Press Ltd,
19-21 Alfred Street,
Belfast BT2 8DL.

MACMILLAN is a trademark of Macmillan, Inc.
Library of Congress Cataloging-in-Publication Data
Shakespeare, William, 1564-1616.
  Othello: shorter Shakespeare/William Shakespeare.
  p. cm.
  ISBN 0-02-861231-0
1. Shakespeare, William, 1564-1616–Adaptations. I. Title.
PR2878.08 1996
822.3′3–dc20   96-17306
                                                    CIP

Printed in Singapore

10 9 8 7 6 5 4 3 2 1

INTRODUCTION

Go back some five hundred years in time; picture yourself in Venice, a city unique then and now. Built upon water, its fragile, beautiful architecture rises over narrow canals, where humpbacked bridges connect a street plan of narrow paths and alleyways. It is a small city, but at this time it is one of the great centers of the known world. Her trading links stretch to Constantinople and far beyond, eastward along the Silk Road to China; southeastward across Egypt to the Spice Islands in the hot Equatorial seas. Her Arsenal and her fleet are crucial weapons to the western world. And that world is under terrible threat - the Turks, who have broken the great empire of the east, are now hammering at the gates of Europe. Venice, with her island possessions in the Mediterranean Sea, is the key. If Venice falls, then the armies of the Crescent will sweep through into the heart of Christian civilization.

Venice is perilously close to defeat. The centuries of strife have depleted her resources. Even her General is not a Venetian by birth, but a mercenary, the North African, Othello. In this strained climate of war and potential disaster, individual fortunes and feelings loom large. Venice has always been a place of plots, of hidden passions. In quiet corners government letterboxes invite secret denunciations of even the most highly placed people in the state. As in a world under the threat of a nuclear annihilation, today is all-important, and tomorrow does not matter. There is no time for careful, strategic planning - decisions must be made fast. The sense of responsibility is a crushing burden for those whose role is to command; they know well that time is not on their side. They also know that within the greater struggle of religions, states, and cultures, individuals are struggling to maintain and defend their honor and reputation.

Under the stress of great events, that individual struggle becomes ever more intense. Violence is never far away, and the dagger is always close to hand. And in this world, where personal honor is paramount and men settle quarrels with their swords, nothing is more important than a woman's sexual fidelity. A wife may be beautiful, accomplished, noble: but if she is known to be unfaithful to her husband, then she is nothing. Her infidelity makes of him a laughingstock, and there is no more shameful thing to any man, let alone a great one. It is against this tense and stormy political and social background that the story of Othello unfolds.

Othello, Moor of Venice, was first performed in 1604.

Othello

Two men are walking in a street in Venice, at dead of night. One is Roderigo, a rich Venetian. His companion, Iago, is a soldier and sharp-minded manipulator. Roderigo had hoped to marry Desdemona, daughter of Brabantio, but Desdemona has secretly married Othello, a Moor, General of the Venetian army. Iago hates the General because he has chosen the inexperienced Michael Cassio to be his second in command. Iago is relegated to being the standard-bearer, which his proud nature takes as an intolerable insult.

IAGO: For when my outward action doth demonstrate

The native act and figure of my heart
In complement extern, 'tis not long after
But I will wear my heart upon my sleeve
For daws to peck at: I am not what I am.

Iago and Roderigo make their way to below Brabantio's windows where they shout for attention until the old man looks out.

IAGO: 'Zounds, sir, y'are robbed; for shame, put on your gown;
Your heart is burst, you have lost half your soul.
Even now, now, very now, an old black ram
Is tupping your white ewe. Arise, arise!

Brabantio, enraged, soon appears at his door, but Iago has already gone. Later Iago informs Othello of Brabantio's fury, but Othello remains calm.

OTHELLO: Let him do his spite.
My services, which I have done the signiory,
Shall out-tongue his complaints.

He is interrupted by the arrival of a group of men. Othello's Lieutenant, Cassio, has come with a summons from the Duke. The war with the Turks has taken a new and dangerous turn and Othello is needed. Brabantio arrives, angry because he thinks Othello has put his daughter under a spell.

BRABANTIO: O thou foul thief, where hast thou stowed my
        daughter?
    Damned as thou art, thou hast enchanted her;

Othello replies that he will answer his accuser in the
Duke's council. When they arrive, Brabantio charges that
his daughter has been stolen away. The Duke is sympa-
thetic and promises revenge once the culprit is identified,
whereupon Brabantio names Othello.

DUKE: Whosoever he be that in this foul proceeding
    Hath thus beguiled your daughter of herself
    And you of her, the bloody book of law
    You shall yourself read in the bitter letter.

BRABANTIO: Humbly I thank your Grace.
    Here is the man, this Moor; whom now, it seems,
    Your special mandate for the state affairs
    Hath hither brought.

Othello responds with a powerful speech in which he
explains that he loves Desdemona and that she is his will-
ing wife.

OTHELLO: Most potent, grave, and reverend signiors,
    My very noble and approved good masters:

That I have taken away this old man's daughter,
It is most true: true, I have married her:
The very head and front of my offending
Hath this extent, no more.

Iago is sent to fetch Desdemona, to test the truth of what Othello has said. Meanwhile, Othello explains to the senators how he wooed Desdemona by telling her about the extraordinary events of his life: how he was sold as a slave and escaped, the battles he fought, and the things he had seen.

OTHELLO: She loved me for the dangers I had passed,
    And I loved her that she did pity them.
    This only is the witchcraft I have used.
    Here comes the lady; let her witness it.

When Desdemona arrives, she addresses her father and tells him that she is torn between respect due to her father and the allegiance she owes her husband.

DESDEMONA: And so much duty as my mother showed
    To you, preferring you before her father,
    So much I challenge that I may profess
    Due to the Moor my lord.

Realizing that Desdemona has married Othello of her own free will, Brabantio grudgingly accepts the situation, and the Council moves on to discuss the Turkish threat to Cyprus. The Duke orders Othello to Cyprus to defend the island.

DUKE: The Turk with a most mighty preparation makes for Cyprus. Othello, the fortitude of the place is best known to you; and though we have there a substitute of most allowed sufficiency, yet opinion, a sovereign mistress of effects, throws a more safer voice on you.

Desdemona pleads to be allowed to accompany her new husband.

DESDEMONA: So that, dear lords, if I be left behind,
    A moth of peace, and he go to the war,
    The rites for which I love him are bereft me,
    And I a heavy interim shall support
    By his dear absence. Let me go with him.

Desdemona's wish is granted, and Roderigo, ever ready to despair, declares that he will drown himself

because Desdemona is lost to him. Iago tells Roderigo that Moors are fickle and prone to changing their minds and advises Roderigo to increase his fortune. Iago promises that Desdemona will soon be Roderigo's.

IAGO: These Moors are changeable in their wills: - fill thy purse with money. The food that to him now is as luscious as locusts shall be to him shortly as bitter as coloquintida. She must change for youth: when she is sated with his body, she will find the error of her choice. She must have change, she must: therefore put money in thy purse.

Roderigo, easily convinced, goes off cheerfully, leaving Iago alone. Another reason for Iago's hatred of Othello now emerges - he has heard a rumor that the Moor has seduced Iago's wife, Emilia. Iago plans to feign loyalty to Othello, believing the Moor will easily be misled.

IAGO: The Moor is of a free and open nature
That thinks men honest that but seem to be so;
And will as tenderly be led by the nose
As asses are.

Before Othello arrives in Cyprus, a storm destroys the Turkish fleet. The threat is passed; they can celebrate. When the General arrives, the Governor is jubilant and Othello is delighted to see his beloved wife.

OTHELLO: Come, let us to the castle.
  News, friends: our wars are done, the Turks are
    drowned.
  How does my old acquaintance of this isle?
  Honey, you shall be well desired in Cyprus:
  I have found great love amongst them.

In the meantime, Iago schemes. His ultimate plan is to
ruin Othello, and he will do so by making it seem that
Cassio and Desdemona are lovers. Knowing Roderigo still
loves Desdemona, Iago repeats the lie to him.

IAGO: Besides, the knave is handsome, young, and hath
  all those requisites in him that folly and green minds
  look after: a pestilent complete knave; and the woman
  hath found him already.

Incensed, Roderigo resolves to pick a fight with Cassio.
To this end Iago appears with a supply of wine, and
invites Cassio to join him for a drink. Cassio refuses at first
but Iago persists, knowing that if Cassio is drunk he will
be more likely to fight when Roderigo challenges him.

IAGO: If I can fasten but one cup upon him,
  With that which he hath drunk to-night already,
  He'll be as full of quarrel and offence
  As my young mistress' dog.

Cassio finally accepts a glass of wine and soon there is a drinking session in progress. In the middle of this Roderigo makes his challenge, and is knocked down by Cassio. The noise of the disturbance brings out Othello. Horrified to see his officers fighting, Othello demands to know the cause. Iago, appearing to defend Cassio, manages to convince Othello that Cassio is the cause of the uproar. Othello thanks Iago for his honesty and then demotes Cassio for his unseemly behavior.

OTHELLO: I know, Iago,
　　Thy honesty and love doth mince this matter,
　　Making it light to Cassio. Cassio, I love thee;
　　But never more be officer of mine.

Iago, ever the hypocrite, consoles the disgraced Cassio, who is horrified by the turn of events.

CASSIO: Reputation, reputation, reputation! O, I have lost my reputation!

Seeing a perfect opportunity to further his plans, Iago offers his advice: Cassio should approach Desdemona and ask her to intercede with Othello on Cassio's behalf, because Othello can refuse his wife nothing.

IAGO: Confess yourself freely to her: importune her help to put you in your place again... This broken joint between you and her husband entreat her to splinter; and, my fortunes against any lay worth naming, this crack of your love shall grow stronger than it was before.

Cassio leaves, and Iago considers his scheme. He intends to make Othello believe that Desdemona is intervening on Cassio's behalf because Cassio is her lover.

IAGO: ... for whiles this honest fool
    Plies Desdemona to repair his fortunes,
    And she for him pleads strongly to the Moor,
    I'll pour this pestilence into his ear,
    That she repeals him for her body's lust;
    And by how much she strives to do him good
    She shall undo her credit with the Moor.
    So will I turn her virtue into pitch;
    And out of her own goodness make the net
    That shall enmesh them all.

After his conversation with Iago, Cassio enlists the help

of Iago's wife, Emilia, who is Desdemona's attendant. Emilia arranges a meeting between Cassio and her mistress. When they meet, Desdemona agrees to support Cassio's reinstatement.

DESDEMONA: Do not doubt that: before Emilia here
    I give thee warrant of thy place. Assure thee,
    If I do vow a friendship, I'll perform it
    To the last article. My lord shall never rest:
    I'll watch him tame and talk him out of patience;
    His bed shall seem a school, his board a shrift;
    I'll intermingle everything he does
    With Cassio's suit. Therefore be merry, Cassio,
    For thy solicitor shall rather die
    Than give thy cause away.

While they are talking, Othello and Iago enter the room, forcing Cassio, who is ashamed to face Othello, to leave the scene. Iago spots Cassio leaving and mutters aloud 'Ha! I like not that,' bringing the matter to Othello's attention.

OTHELLO: Was not that Cassio parted from my wife?

IAGO: Cassio, my lord! No, sure, I cannot think it,
    That he would sneak away so guilty-like,
    Seeing you coming.

OTHELLO: I do believe 'twas he.

Desdemona then begins to plead for Cassio's return to favor. Othello's patronizing attitude causes Desdemona to rebuke him.

DESDEMONA: Why, this is not a boon:
   'Tis as I should entreat you wear your gloves,
   Or feed on nourishing dishes, or keep you warm,
   Or sue to you to do a peculiar profit
   To your own person. Nay, when I have a suit
   Wherein I mean to touch your love indeed,
   It shall be full of poise and difficult weight,
   And fearful to be granted.

After Desdemona leaves, Iago embarks on the most difficult part of his design - making Othello suspect the

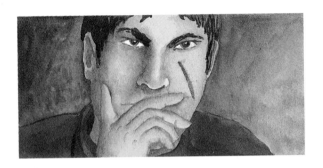

person he most dearly loves. He asks Othello if Cassio knew Desdemona before their marriage. When the general replies that Cassio had often been their go-between, Iago's comment, 'Discernest thou aught in that?', and his shrugs, indirect hints, and protests of love and loyalty to Othello, begin to make Othello suspicious. The crafty Iago even counsels Othello not to be jealous.

IAGO: O, beware, my lord, of jealousy:
　　It is the green-eyed monster, which doth mock
　　The meat it feeds on. That cuckold lives in bliss
　　Who, certain of his fate, loves not his wronger;
　　But, O, what damned minutes tells he over
　　Who dotes, yet doubts, suspects, yet strongly loves!

Othello, despite his pride and insecurity, is not one to make a hasty judgement based on such vague, if alarming, information as Iago has provided. But he is concerned enough to ask to be shown hard evidence of Desdemona's unfaithfulness.

OTHELLO: No, Iago, I'll see before I doubt; when I doubt, prove;
And on the proof, there is no more but this:
Away at once with love or jealousy!

As Iago senses his slander take hold, his boldness increases. Meanwhile Othello, devastated by Iago's insinuations, pretends not to be troubled.

IAGO: I see this hath a little dashed your spirits.

OTHELLO: Not a jot, not a jot.

When Iago departs, Othello ponders their conversation, never suspecting that Iago is motivated by anything other than loyalty. Cursing his marriage, Othello laments his misfortune.

OTHELLO: This fellow's of exceeding honesty,
And knows all qualities, with a learned spirit,
Of human dealings. If I do prove her haggard,
Though that her jesses were my dear heart-strings,
I'd whistle her off and let her down the wind
To prey at fortune. Haply, for I am black

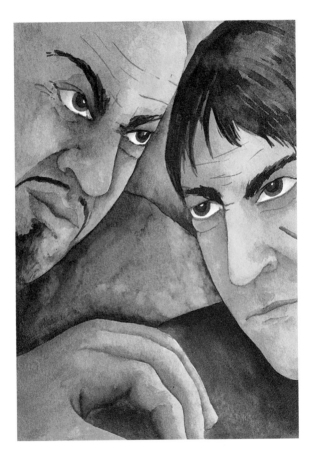

And have not those soft parts of conversation
That chamberers have, or for I am declined
Into the vale of years, - yet that's not much
She's gone; I am abused, and my relief
Must be to loathe her. O curse of marriage,
That we can call these delicate creatures ours,
And not their appetites! I had rather be a toad,
And live upon the vapour of a dungeon,
Than keep a corner in the thing I love
For others' uses.

When Desdemona joins Othello she notices his pained expression. He makes the excuse of having a headache. Desdemona tries to tie her handkerchief around it, but it is too small and falls off. Emilia picks it up. As soon as Iago sees it, he snatches it from her. He will place the handkerchief in Cassio's room, knowing that when Othello sees Cassio with it, he will recognize it as Desdemona's and take it as proof of her infidelity.

IAGO: I will in Cassio's lodging lose this napkin,
And let him find it. Trifles light as air
Are to the jealous confirmations strong
As proofs of holy writ. This may do something.
The Moor already changes with my poison:

When Iago next meets Othello, he is greeted with hostility. Othello tells him he has been plagued with doubt since Iago brought the matter of Cassio to his attention. Othello goes on to say that he would rather have not known than be tortured this way.

OTHELLO: Avaunt! Be gone! Thou hast set me on the rack.
  I swear 'tis better to be much abused
  Than but to know a little...
  I had been happy if the general camp,
  Pioneers and all, had tasted her sweet body,
  So I had no thing known. O, now for ever
  Farewell the tranquil mind! farewell content!

Othello warns Iago of what lies in store if his insinuations prove false.

OTHELLO: Villain, be sure thou prove my love a whore!
  Be sure of it; give me the ocular proof!
  Or, by the worth of a man's eternal soul,
  Thou hadst been better have been born a dog
  Than answer my waked wrath!

The subtle Iago claims to be an honest man.

IAGO: To be direct and honest is not safe.
  I thank you for this profit and from hence
  I'll love no friend since love breeds such offence.

Othello then confesses his agonizing doubts. He is torn

between believing Iago or Desdemona.

OTHELLO: By the world,
I think my wife be honest, and think she is not;
I think that thou art just, and think thou art not.
I'll have some proof.

Cruel Iago now invents a story of Cassio talking in his sleep.

IAGO: There are a kind of men so loose of soul
That in their sleeps will mutter their affairs.
One of this kind is Cassio.
In sleep I heard him say 'Sweet Desdemona,
Let us be wary, let us hide our loves;'
And then, sir, would he gripe and wring my hand,
Cry 'O sweet creature!' and then kiss me hard,
As if he plucked up kisses by the roots,
That grew upon my lips. Then laid his leg
Over my thigh, and sighed, and kissed, and then

Cried 'Cursed fate that gave thee to the Moor!'

OTHELLO: O montrous! Monstrous!

Finally Iago delivers the final bit of "proof" of Desdmona's infidelity - the handkerchief.

IAGO: Tell me but this:
  Have you not sometimes seen a handkerchief
  Spotted with strawberries in your wife's hand?

OTHELLO: I gave her such a one: 'twas my first gift.

IAGO: I know not that: but such a handkerchief
  I am sure it was your wife's - did I to-day
  See Cassio wipe his beard with.

OTHELLO: O, that the slave had forty thousand lives!
  One is too poor, too weak for my revenge.
  Now do I see 'tis true. Look here, Iago:
  All my fond love thus do I blow to heaven.
  'Tis gone.
  Arise, black vengeance, from the hollow hell!
  Yield up, O love, thy crown and hearted throne
  To tyrannous hate!

Thus deceived, Othello solemnly shakes hands with Iago and orders him to kill Cassio. Now Iago cunningly suggests that Desdemona be spared, thus putting the

very idea of her destruction into Othello's head. Othello refuses and declares that Desdemona, too, must die. He tells Iago to arrange some way of killing Desdemona and then appoints him his Lieutenant.

OTHELLO: Damn her, lewd minx! O, damn her!
   Come, go with me apart: I will withdraw,
   To furnish me with some swift means of death
   For the fair devil. Now art thou my Lieutenant.

IAGO: I am your own forever.

When Desdemona discovers that her handkerchief is missing she knows that Othello will be very upset, because it was his first gift to her. Her fears are realized when Othello asks her to lend him her handkerchief.

DESDEMONA: Here, my lord.

OTHELLO: That which I gave you.

DESDEMONA: I have it not about me.

OTHELLO: Not?

DESDEMONA: No, faith, my lord.

OTHELLO: That's a fault. That handkerchief
    Did an Egyptian to my mother give:
    She was a charmer, and could almost read
    The thoughts of people. She told her, while she kept it
    It would make her amiable and subdue my father
    Entirely to her love, but if she lost it
    Or made a gift of it, my father's eye
    Should hold her loathed and his spirits should hunt
    After new fancies. She dying gave it me,
    And bid me, when my fate would have me wived,
    To give it her. I did so: and take heed on it;
    Make it a darling like your precious eye;
    To lose it or give it away were such perdition
    As nothing else could match.

Desdemona, frightened by her husband's intensity of
feeling, tells him that the handkerchief is not lost. He
orders her to get it. Trying to lighten the atmosphere she

innocently suggests that her husband is trying to change the subject from Cassio's reinstatement. Unable to control his anger, Othello storms off, leaving Desdemona wondering what she has done wrong.

DESDEMONA: Sure there's some wonder in this handker-
        chief.
   I am most unhappy in the loss of it.

Iago brings Cassio again to Desdemona to see how she has fared in pleading his case. The young wife explains that her pleading has had no effect on her husband and also confesses her worries about losing Othello's favor. She can only hope that it is affairs of state that have distracted him.

DESDEMONA: Something sure of state,
   Either from Venice or some unhatched practice
   Made monstrable here in Cyprus to him,
   Hath puddled his clear spirit.

When Cassio later finds the handkerchief in his room, he shows it to Bianca, a local prostitute who has become his mistress. Taken by the design, Cassio asks Bianca to copy it for him before the owner comes to claim it. Meanwhile, Iago takes every opportunity to increase Othello's jealousy.

OTHELLO: Think so, Iago?

IAGO: What! To kiss in private?

OTHELLO: An unauthorised kiss.

IAGO: Or to be naked with her friend in bed
An hour or more, not meaning any harm?

OTHELLO: Naked in bed, Iago, and not mean harm!

Iago continues until Othello has a fit in which he loses consciousness. When Othello comes to, Iago persuades him to hide while Iago and Cassio are talking. Iago steers the conversation to Bianca, knowing that Othello will assume that Cassio is discussing Desdemona.

IAGO: As he shall smile, Othello shall go mad;
And his unbookish jealousy must construe
Poor Cassio's smiles, gestures and light behaviour,
Quite in the wrong.

Othello's jealousy increases as he eavesdrops, thinking Cassio is bragging about how Desdemona throws herself at him.

CASSIO: She was here even now. She haunts me in every place. I was the other day talking on the sea-bank with certain Venetians; and thither comes the bauble, and,

by this hand, she falls on me thus about my neck -

OTHELLO: Crying 'O dear Cassio!' as it were, his gesture
imports it.

Bianca then arrives and turns on her lover for asking
her to make a copy of the handkerchief, because she
thinks it belongs to a rival for Cassio's affections. She does
not realize that she is confirming Desdemona's and
Cassio's "guilt" to the eavesdropping Othello.

BIANCA: A likely piece of work that you should find it in
your chamber and know not who left it there! This is
some minx's token, and I must take out the work?
There: give it your hobby-horse. Wheresoever you had
it, I'll take out no work on't.

After Bianca and Cassio leave, Othello asks Iago if it
was Desdemona's handkerchief.

IAGO: Yours, by his hand: and to see how he prizes the
foolish woman your wife! She gave it him, and he hath

given it his whore.

OTHELLO: I would have him nine years a-killing.
A fine woman! a fair woman! a sweet woman!

IAGO: Nay, you must forget that.

OTHELLO: Ay, let her rot, and perish, and be damned
tonight; for she shall not live. No, my heart is turned to
stone: I strike it, and it hurts my hand. O, the world
hath not a sweeter creature: she might lie by an emp-
eror's side, and command him tasks.

Seeing that Othello is now torn between love for his
wife and the "evidence" of her adultery, Iago suggests
that perhaps if Othello loves Desdemona so very much
maybe he can overlook her indiscretion and turn a blind
eye to her affair. This rekindles Othello's rage.

IAGO: If you are so fond over her iniquity, give her patent
to offend; for, if it touch not you, it comes near nobody.

OTHELLO: I will chop her into messes. Cuckold me!

IAGO: O, 'tis foul in her.

OTHELLO: With mine officer!

IAGO: That's fouler.

Othello orders Iago to get some poison to kill Desdemona. She will die that very night. But Iago has another suggestion.

OTHELLO: Get me some poison, Iago: this night. I'll not expostulate with her, lest her body and beauty unprovide my mind again. This night, Iago.

IAGO: Do it not with poison, strangle her in her bed, even the bed she hath contaminated.

OTHELLO: Good, good! The justice of it pleases: very good.

Desdemona's kinsman, Lodovico, arrives as a messenger from the Duke in Venice commanding Othello to return to Venice, and appointing Cassio Governor of Cyprus. Obsessed with the question of Desdemona's infidelity, Othello pays little heed to Lodovico and leaves to interrogate Emilia.

OTHELLO: You are welcome sir to Cyprus - goats and monkeys. (*Exits*)

LODOVICO: Is this the noble Moor whom our full senate
Call all-in-all sufficient? Is this the nature
Whom passion could not shake? Whose solid virtue
The shot of accident nor dart of chance

Could neither graze or pierce?

IAGO: He is much chang'd.

Meanwhile, Emilia resolutely defends Desdemona's virtue. But when Desdemona comes to Othello and he asks 'What art thou?', Desdemona's answer, 'Your wife, my lord, your true and loyal wife', only rouses him to new rage.

OTHELLO: Swear thou art honest.

DESDEMONA: Heaven doth truly know it.

OTHELLO: Heaven truly knows that thou art false as hell.

DESDEMONA: To whom, my lord? With whom? How am I false?

OTHELLO: O Desdemona! Away! away! away!

Aware that in some unfathomable way she has offended Othello, Desdemona pleads with her husband.

DESDEMONA: Alas, what ignorant sin have I committed?

OTHELLO: Was this fair paper, this most goodly book,
Made to write 'whore' upon? What committed!
Committed! O thou public commoner!
I should make very forges of my cheeks
That would to cinders burn up modesty,
Did I but speak thy deeds. What committed!
Heaven stops the nose at it, and the moon winks;
The bawdy wind, that kisses all it meets,
Is hushed within the hollow mine of earth
And will not hear it. What committed!
Impudent strumpet!

Mystified, afraid, and deeply hurt, Desdemona can think of no one to advise her in her difficulty but Iago, and so she sends Emilia to find him. Iago feigns concern and horror about what has taken place, but Emilia guesses the truth of the matter.

EMILIA: I will be hanged if some eternal villain,
Some busy and insinuating rogue,
Some cogging, cozening slave, to get some office,

Have not devised this slander. I'll be hanged else.

IAGO: Fie, there is no such man: it is impossible.

Desdemona's only thought is to regain Othello's love. She turns to Iago for advice.

DESDEMONA: O good Iago, What shall I do to win my lord
      again?
  Good friend, go to him; for, by this light of heaven,
  I know not how I lost him. Here I kneel:
  If ever my will did trespass against his love
  Either in discourse of thought or actual deed,
  Or that mine eyes, mine ears, or any sense,
  Delighted them in any other form,
  Or that I do not yet, and ever did,
  And ever will, though he do shake me off
  To beggarly divorcement, love him dearly,
  Comfort forswear me!

She is interrupted in her declaration by trumpets summoning her to a formal dinner with Othello and Lodovico. Iago is then approached by Roderigo, who agrees to kill Cassio, so that Othello, and therefore Desdemona, will be forced to stay on in Cyprus.

IAGO: He goes into Mauritania, and takes away with him
  the fair Desdemona, unless his abode be lingered here

by some accident, wherein none can be so determinate as the removing of Cassio.

RODERIGO: How do you mean, removing him?

IAGO: Why by making him uncapable of Othello's place: knocking out his brains.

RODERIGO: And that you would have me do?

Later, as Desdemona is preparing for bed, she speaks to Emilia about her concern for Othello.

EMILIA: I would you had never seen him!

DESDEMONA: So would not I. My love doth so approve him
That even his stubbornness, his checks, his frowns,
Prithee unpin me, - have grace and favour in them.

Desdemona then asks Emilia if she thinks that some women would be unfaithful to their husbands. Emilia says that there are indeed such women. Desdemona is

shocked and declares that nothing could ever persuade her be unfaithful to her husband.

DESDEMONA: Beshrew me, if I would do such a wrong
    For the whole world.

And so night descends, but without quietness or peace. Roderigo, a reluctant assassin, is set to ambush Cassio. When Cassio comes along, Roderigo makes a clumsy lunge at him, but Cassio manages to draw his sword and strike down his assailant. Forced to intervene, Iago stabs Cassio from behind, slashing a deep wound in his leg, before running off. Then, the ever-treacherous Iago kills Roderigo so that he will not disclose the plan. Iago leaves, then returns, pretending to have just come upon the scene.

IAGO: I cry you mercy. Here's Cassio hurt by villains.

GRATIANO: Cassio!

IAGO: How is it, brother?

CASSIO: My leg is cut in two.

IAGO: Marry, heaven forbid!
    Light, gentlemen: I'll bind it with my shirt.

Meanwhile, in Desdemona's bedroom, the events of

the night outside have not been heard. She is asleep as
Othello enters the room. He comes to her bedside and
kisses her. She does not hear him confess that he will
always love her even after he has murdered her.

OTHELLO: O balmy breath, that dost almost persuade
   Justice to break her sword! One more, one more.
   Be thus when thou art dead, and I will kill thee,
   And love thee after. One more, and that's the last:
   So sweet was never so fatal. I must weep,
   But they are cruel tears. This sorrow's heavenly:
   It strikes where it doth love.

DESDEMONA: Will you come to bed, my lord?

OTHELLO: Have you prayed tonight, Desdemona? ...
   I would not kill thy unprepared spirit;

No, heaven forfend! I would not kill thy soul.

Terrified, Desdemona asks her husband what she has done to turn him so violently against her. Othello tells her that he knows she is having an affair with Cassio and that she has given Othello's gift to her lover.

OTHELLO: That handkerchief which I so loved and gave thee
Thou gavest to Cassio.

Desdemona pleads for Cassio to be called to confirm her innocence. But when Othello tells her Cassio is dead, she sees her last hope is gone. Her final plea is for more time:

DESDEMONA: Kill me tomorrow: let me live to-night!

OTHELLO: Nay, if you strive...

DESDEMONA: But half an hour!

OTHELLO: Being done, there is no pause.

DESDEMONA: But while I say one prayer!

OTHELLO: It is too late.

Othello then smothers Desdemona with a pillow, but as he does so, Emilia calls to him from outside the room,

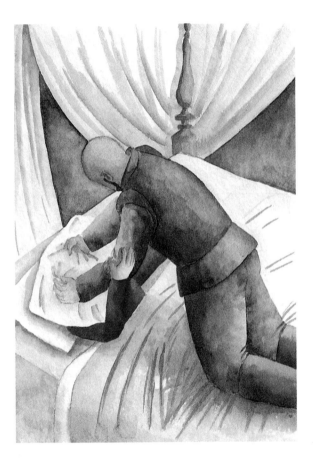

interrupting him.

OTHELLO: Yes: 'tis Emilia. By and by. She's dead.
  'Tis like she comes to speak of Cassio's death.
  The noise was here. Ha! no more moving?
  Still as the grave. Shall she come in? Were it good?
  I think she stirs again. No. What's best to do?
  If she come in, she'll sure speak to my wife.
  My wife! my wife! What wife? I have no wife.
  O, insupportable! O heavy hour!

Like a man in a dream, Othello unlocks the door and
Emilia tumbles in, with the news of the fight outside.
Othello receives the news wearily, until she tells him that
Cassio is alive.

EMILIA: No, Cassio is not killed.

OTHELLO: Not Cassio killed! Then murder's out of tune,
  And sweet revenge grows harsh.

In the middle of this confusion, Desdemona's voice is
heard, faintly, protesting her innocence with her last
breath. Emilia is distraught and asks Desdemona who has
attacked her. Despite his cruelty, Desdemona tries to pro-
tect Othello and tells Emilia that she has brought her
death upon herself.

DESDEMONA: A guiltless death I die.

EMILIA: O, who hath done this deed?

DESDEMONA: Nobody: I myself. Farewell.
    Commend me to my kind lord. O, farewell!

Othello tells Emilia that Desdemona has been unfaithful and that Emilia's husband, Iago, was a witness to Desdemona's treachery.

OTHELLO: Cassio did tup her: ask thy husband else.
    O, I were damned beneath all depth in hell
    But that I did proceed upon just grounds
    To this extremity. Thy husband knew it all.

EMILIA: My husband?

OTHELLO: Thy husband.

EMILIA: O gull! O dolt!
    As ignorant as dirt! Thou hast done a deed -
    I care not for thy sword: I'll make thee known,
    Though I lost twenty lives. Help! help, ho! help!
    The Moor hath killed my mistress! Murder! murder!

Emilia's screams bring in the others and she turns upon her husband, Iago, accusing him of telling lies and being responsible for an innocent woman's death.

EMILIA: You told a lie, an odious, damned lie;
    Upon my soul, a lie, a wicked lie!
    She false with Cassio! Did you say with Cassio?

IAGO: With Cassio, mistress. Go to, charm your tongue.

EMILIA: I will not charm my tongue: I am bound to speak:
    My mistress here lies murdered in her bed.

ALL: O heavens forfend!

EMILIA: And your reports have set the murder on.

Ever defiant, Othello states again his reasons for murdering his wife.

OTHELLO: 'Tis pitiful, but yet Iago knows
    That she with Cassio hath the act of shame
    A thousand times committed: Cassio confessed it.
    And she did gratify his amorous works
    With that recognisance and pledge of love
    Which I first gave her: I saw it in his hand.
    It was a handkerchief, an antique token

My father gave my mother.

Despite Iago's frenzied attempts to hush her, Emilia tells how she found the handkerchief and how Iago took it from her. Iago rushes at Emilia and stabs her. Othello, realizing he has killed the woman he loves on the strength of lies and fabricated evidence, is devastated. He tries to stab Iago, but is restrained by his officers. Emilia's dying words are a bitter rebuke to Othello.

EMILIA: Moor, she was chaste; she loved thee, cruel Moor.

All the officers then gather in Desdemona's room and Lodovico takes charge of the proceedings. Othello tells the court that he has murdered in the name of honor.

LODOVICO: O thou Othello, that was once so good,
    Fallen in the practice of a damned slave,
    What shall be said to thee?

OTHELLO: Why, anything.
    An honourable murderer, if you will;
    For nought I did in hate, but all in honour.

LODOVICO: This wretch hath in part confessed his villainy:
    Did you and he consent in Cassio's death?

OTHELLO: Ay.

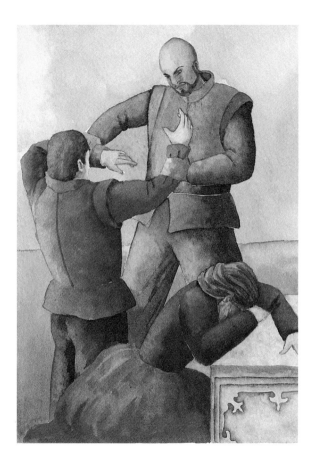

CASSIO: Dear General, I never gave you cause.

OTHELLO: I do believe it, and I ask your pardon.
Will you, I pray, demand that demi-devil
Why he hath thus ensnared my soul and body?

IAGO: Demand me nothing: what you know, you know.
From this time forth I never will speak word.

Lodovico slowly states what must be done. Cassio will
act as Governor in Cyprus. Iago will be taken away to be
executed. Othello will be taken back to Venice for trial.
Othello asks that his tale be told truthfully - neither exag-
gerated nor underplayed.

OTHELLO: Soft you: a word or two before you go.
I have done the state some service, and they know it.

No more of that. I pray you, in your letters,
When you shall these unlucky deeds relate,
Speak of me as I am; nothing extenuate,
Nor set down aught in malice. Then must you speak
Of one that loved not wisely but too well;
... I kissed thee ere I killed thee. No way but this,
Killing myself, to die upon a kiss. (*Stabs himself*)

CASSIO: This I did fear, but thought he had no weapon;
For he was great of heart.

LODOVICO: Myself will straight aboard, and to the state
This heavy act with heavy heart relate.

Dawn breaks and the three bodies are taken up by
Othello's officers and carried offstage: tragic victims of
Iago's evil and poisoned mind.

GLOSSARY

The Moor: from Mauritania, in North Africa

`zounds:  abbreviation of `God's Wounds': a swear-word

tupping: mating with (as of animals)

sagittary: the sign of Sagittarius, over Othello's house.

signiory: the government of Venice

unbonneted: not inferior

coloquintida: a bitter-tasting drug

pitch: black tar

shrift: a confessional

cuckold: a deceived husband

haggard: a wild hawk

jesses: the hawk's restraints

let her down the wind: let the hawk fly free

Dian's visage: the face of the goddess Diana

charmer: a magician

such a deed: adultery